NEW & SELECTED POEMS, 1940–1986

NEW & SELECTED POEMS, 1940–1986

Karl Shapiro

The University of Chicago Press
Chicago & London

The University of Chicago Press, Chicago 60637
The University of Chicago Press, Ltd., London
© 1987 by Karl Shapiro
All Rights reserved. Published 1987
Printed in the United States of America

96 95 94 93 92 91 90 89 88   5 4 3 2

Library of Congress Cataloging in Publication Data

Shapiro, Karl Jay, 1913–
    New & Selected poems, 1940–1986.

    I. Title.   II. Title: New and selected poems, 1940–
1986.
PS3537.H27A6   1987   811'.52   87–10790
ISBN 0–226–75033–7 (pbk.)

KARL SHAPIRO has taught at the Johns Hopkins
University, the University of Nebraska, and, until his
recent retirement, the University of California, Davis.
A past editor of *Poetry* and *Prairie Schooner,* he is the
author of numerous volumes of poetry, including
*Person, Place and Thing; The Bourgeois Poet; Adult
Bookstore;* and *Collected Poems 1940–1978* as well as
several critical studies and a film, "Karl Shapiro's
America."

To Sophie

Roses in late November
Here where the skies begin
Bring poetry back to love.
Thank you for bringing them in.

Contents

The Dome of Sunday

With focus sharp as Flemish-painted face
In film of varnish brightly fixed
And through a polished hand-lens deeply seen,
Sunday at noon through hyaline thin air
Sees down the street,
And in the camera of my eye depicts
Row-houses and row-lives:
Glass after glass, door after door the same,
Face after face the same, the same,
The brutal visibility the same;

As if one life emerging from one house
Would pause, a single image caught between
Two facing mirrors where vision multiplies
Beyond perspective,
A silent clatter in the high-speed eye
Spinning out photo-circulars of sight.

I see slip to the curb the long machines
Out of whose warm and windowed rooms pirouette
Shellacked with silk and light
The hard legs of our women.
Our women are one woman, dressed in black.
The carmine printed mouth
And cheeks as soft as muslin-glass belong
Outright to one dark dressy man,
Merely a swagger at her curvy side.
This is their visit to themselves:
All day from porch to porch they weave
A nonsense pattern through the even glare,
Stealing in surfaces
Cold vulgar glances at themselves.

And high up in the heated room all day
I wait behind the plate glass pane for one,
Hot as a voyeur for a glimpse of one,
The vision to blot out this woman's sheen;

All day my sight records expensively
Row-houses and row-lives.

But nothing happens; no diagonal
With melting shadow falls across the curb:
Neither the blinded negress lurching through fatigue,
Nor exiles bleeding from their pores,
Nor that bright bomb slipped lightly from its rack
To splinter every silvered glass and crystal prism,
Witch-bowl and perfume bottle
And billion candle-power dressing-bulb,
No direct hit to smash the shatter-proof
And lodge at last the quivering needle
Clean in the eye of one who stands transfixed
In fascination of her brightness.

Washington Cathedral

From summer and the wheel-shaped city
That sweats like a swamp and wrangles on
Its melting streets, white mammoth Forums,
And political hotels with awnings, caryatids;
Past barricaded embassies with trees
That shed trash and parch his eyes,
To here, the acres of superior quiet,
Shadow and damp, the tourist comes,
And, cooled by stones and darkness, stares.

Tall as a lover's night, the nave
Broods over him, irradiates,
And stars of color out of painted glass
Shoot downward on apostles and on chairs
Huddled by hundreds under altar rails.
Yet it is only Thursday; there are no prayers,

But exclamations. The lady invokes by name
The thousand-odd small sculptures, spooks,
New angels, pitted roods; she gives
The inventory of relics to his heart
That aches with history and astonishment:
He gives a large coin to a wooden coffer.

Outside, noon blazes in his face like guns.
He goes down by the Bishop's walk, the dial,
The expensive grass, the Byzantine bench,
While stark behind him a red naked crane
Hangs over the unfinished transept,
A Cubist hen rivalling the Gothic School.

Whether he sees the joke; whether he cares;
Whether he tempts a vulgar miracle,
Some deus ex machina, this is his choice,
A shrine of whispers and tricky penumbras.
Therefore he votes again for the paid

Clergy, the English hint, the bones of Wilson
Crushed under tons of fake magnificence.
        Nor from the zoo of his instincts
        Come better than crude eagles: now
He cannot doubt that violent obelisk
And Lincoln whittled to a fool's colossus.
This church and city triumph in his eyes.
He is only a good alien, nominally happy.

Hospital

Inside or out, the key is pain. It holds
The florist to your pink medicinal rose,
The nickname to the corpse. One wipes it from
Blue German blades or drops it down the drain;
The novelist with a red tube up his nose
Gingerly pets it. Nurse can turn it off.

This is the Oxford of all sicknesses.
Kings have lain here and fabulous small Jews
And actresses whose legs were always news.
In this black room the painter lost his sight,
The crippled dancer here put down her shoes,
And the scholar's memory broke, like an old clock.

These reached to heaven and inclined their heads
While starchy angels reached them into beds:
These stooped to hell to labor out their time,
Or choked to death in seas of glaucous slime:
All tasted fire, and then, their hate annealed,
Ate sad ice-cream and wept upon a child.

What church is this, what factory of souls
Makes the bad good and fashions a new nose,
And the doctors reel with Latin and even the dead
Expect the unexpected? For O the souls
Fly back like heavy homing-birds to roost
In long-racked limbs, filling the lonely boughs.

The dead cry *life* and stagger up the hill;
But is there still the incorrigible city where
The well enjoy their poverty and the young
Worship the gutter? Is Wednesday still alive
And Tuesday wanting terribly to sin?
Hush, there are many pressing the oak doors,

Saying, "Are boys and girls important fears?
Can you predict the elections by my guts?"

But the rubber gloves are deep in a deep wound,
Stitching a single heart. These far surpass
Themselves, their wives, and the removed goitre;
Are, for the most part, human but unbandaged.

Auto Wreck

Its quick soft silver bell beating, beating,
And down the dark one ruby flare
Pulsing out red light like an artery,
The ambulance at top speed floating down
Past beacons and illuminated clocks
Wings in a heavy curve, dips down,
And brakes speed, entering the crowd.
The doors leap open, emptying light;
Stretchers are laid out, the mangled lifted
And stowed into the little hospital.
Then the bell, breaking the hush, tolls once,
And the ambulance with its terrible cargo
Rocking, slightly rocking, moves away,
As the doors, an afterthought, are closed.

We are deranged, walking among the cops
Who sweep glass and are large and composed.
One is still making notes under the light.
One with a bucket douches ponds of blood
Into the street and gutter.
One hangs lanterns on the wrecks that cling,
Empty husks of locusts, to iron poles.

Our throats were tight as tourniquets,
Our feet were bound with splints, but now,
Like convalescents intimate and gauche,
We speak through sickly smiles and warn
With the stubborn saw of common sense,
The grim joke and the banal resolution.
The traffic moves around with care,
But we remain, touching a wound
That opens to our richest horror.
Already old, the question Who shall die?
Becomes unspoken Who is innocent?
For death in war is done by hands;
Suicide has cause and stillbirth, logic;
And cancer, simple as a flower, blooms.

But this invites the occult mind,
Cancels our physics with a sneer,
And spatters all we knew of denouement
Across the expedient and wicked stones.

The Fly

O hideous little bat, the size of snot,
With polyhedral eye and shabby clothes,
To populate the stinking cat you walk
The promontory of the dead man's nose,
Climb with the fine leg of a Duncan-Phyfe
    The smoking mountains of my food
        And in a comic mood
In mid-air take to bed a wife.

Riding and riding with your filth of hair
On gluey feet or wing, forever coy,
Hot from the compost and green sweet decay,
Sounding your buzzer like an urchin toy—
You dot all whiteness with diminutive stool,
    In the tight belly of the dead
        Burrow with hungry head
And inlay maggots like a jewel.

At your approach the great horse stomps and paws
Bringing the hurricane of his heavy tail;
Shod in disease you dare to kiss my hand
Which sweeps against you like an angry flail;
Still you return, return, trusting your wing
    To draw you from the hunter's reach
        That learns to kill to teach
Disorder to the tinier thing.

My peace is your disaster. For your death
Children like spiders cup their pretty hands
And wives resort to chemistry of war.
In fens of sticky paper and quicksands
You glue yourself to death. Where you are stuck
    You struggle hideously and beg,
        You amputate your leg
Imbedded in the amber muck.

But I, a man, must swat you with my hate,
Slap you across the air and crush your flight,
Must mangle with my shoe and smear your blood,
Expose your little guts pasty and white,
Knock your head sidewise like a drunkard's hat,
    Pin your wings under like a crow's,
        Tear off your flimsy clothes
And beat you as one beats a rat.

Then like Gargantua I stride among
The corpses strewn like raisins in the dust,
The broken bodies of the narrow dead
That catch the throat with fingers of disgust.
I sweep. One gyrates like a top and falls
    And stunned, stone blind, and deaf
        Buzzes its frightful F
And dies between three cannibals.

Drug Store

I do remember an apothecary,
And hereabouts 'a dwells

It baffles the foreigner like an idiom,
And he is right to adopt it as a form
Less serious than the living-room or bar;
    For it disestablishes the café,
Is a collective, and on basic country.

Not that it praises hygiene and corrupts
The ice-cream parlor and the tobacconist's
Is it a center; but that the attractive symbols
    Watch over puberty and leer
Like rubber bottles waiting for sick-use.

Youth comes to jingle nickels and crack wise;
The baseball scores are his, the magazines
Devoted to lust, the jazz, the Coca-Cola,
    The lending-library of love's latest.
He is the customer; he is heroized.

And every nook and cranny of the flesh
Is spoken to by packages with wiles.
"Buy me, buy me," they whimper and cajole;
    The hectic range of lipstick pouts,
Revealing the wicked and the simple mouth.

With scarcely any evasion in their eye
They smoke, undress their girls, exact a stance;
But only for a moment. The clock goes round;
    Crude fellowships are made and lost;
They slump in booths like rags, not even drunk.

Waitress

Whoever with the compasses of his eyes
Is plotting the voyage of your steady shape
As you come laden through the room and back
And rounding your even bottom like a Cape
Crooks his first finger, whistles through his lip
Till you arrive, all motion, like a ship,

He is my friend—consider his dark pangs
And love of Niger, naked indigence,
Dance him the menu of a poem and squirm
Deep in the juke-box jungle, green and dense.
Surely he files his teeth, punctures his nose,
Carves out the god and takes off all his clothes.

For once, the token on the table's edge
Sufficing, proudly and with hair unpinned
You mounted the blueplate, stretched out and grinned
Like Christmas fish and turkey pink and skinned,
Eyes on the half-shell, loin with parsley stuck,
Thigh-bones and ribs and little toes to suck.

I speak to you, ports of the northern myth,
This dame is carved and eaten. One by one,
God knows what hour, her different parts go home,
Lastly her pants, and day or night is done;
But on the restaurant the sign of fear
Reddens and blazes—"English spoken here."

University

To hurt the Negro and avoid the Jew
Is the curriculum. In mid-September
The entering boys, identified by hats,
Wander in a maze of mannered brick
    Where boxwood and magnolia brood
    And columns with imperious stance
    Like rows of ante-bellum girls
        Eye them, outlanders.

In whited cells, on lawns equipped for peace,
Under the arch, and lofty banister,
Equals shake hands, unequals blankly pass;
The exemplary weather whispers, "Quiet, quiet"
    And visitors on tiptoe leave
    For the raw North, the unfinished West,
    As the young, detecting an advantage,
        Practice a face.

Where, on their separate hill, the colleges,
Like manor houses of an older law,
Gaze down embankments on a land in fee,
The Deans, dry spinsters over family plate,
    Ring out the English name like coin,
    Humor the snob and lure the lout.
    Within the precincts of this world
        Poise is a club.

But on the neighboring range, misty and high,
The past is absolute: some luckless race
Dull with inbreeding and conformity
Wears out its heart, and comes barefoot and bad
    For charity or jail. The scholar
    Sanctions their obsolete disease;
    The gentleman revolts with shame
        At his ancestor.

And the true nobleman, once a democrat,
Sleeps on his private mountain. He was one
Whose thought was shapely and whose dream was broad;
This school he held his art and epitaph.
　　But now it takes from him his name,
　　Falls open like a dishonest look,
　　And shows us, rotted and endowed,
　　　　Its senile pleasure.

Haircut

O wonderful nonsense of lotions of Lucky Tiger,
Of savory soaps and oils of bottle-bright green,
The gold of liqueurs, the unguents of Newark and Niger,
Powders and balms and waters washing me clean;

In mirrors of marble and silver I see us forever
Increasing, decreasing the puzzles of luminous spaces,
As I turn, am revolved and am pumped in the air on a lever,
With the backs of my heads in chorus with all of my faces.

Scissors and comb are mowing my hair into neatness,
Now pruning my ears, now smoothing my neck like a plain;
In the harvest of hair and the chaff of powdery sweetness
My snow-covered slopes grow dark with the wooly rain.

And the little boy cries, for it hurts to sever the curl,
And we too are quietly bleating to part with our coat.
Does the barber want blood in a dish? I am weak as a girl,
I desire my pendants, the fatherly chin of a goat.

I desire the pants of a bear, the nap of a monkey
Which trousers of friction have blighted down to my skin.
I am bare as a tusk, as jacketed up as a flunkey,
With the chest of a moth-eaten camel growing within.

But in death we shall flourish, you summer-dark leaves of
    my head,
While the flesh of the jaw ebbs away from the shores of my
    teeth;
You shall cover my sockets and soften the boards of my bed
And lie on the flat of my temples as proud as a wreath.

Mongolian Idiot

A dog that spoke, a monster born of sheep
We mercilessly kill, and kill the thought,
Yet house the parrot and let the centaur go,
These being to their nature and those not.
We laugh at apes, that never quite succeed
      At eating soup or wearing hats.

Adam had named so many but not this,
This that would name a curse when it had come,
Unfinished man, or witch, or myth, or sin,
Not ever father and never quite a son.
Ape had outstripped him, dog and darling lamb
      And all the kindergarten beasts.

Enter the bare room of his mind and count
His store of words with letters large and black;
See how he handles clumsily those blocks
With swans and sums; his colored picture books.
At thirty-five he squeals to see the ball
    Bounce in the air and roll away.

Pity and fear we give this innocent
Who maimed his mother's beautiful instinct;
But she would say, "My body had a dog;
I bore the ape and nursed the crying sheep.
He is my kindness and my splendid gift
      Come from all life and for all life."

Buick

As a sloop with a sweep of immaculate wing on her delicate
  spine
And a keel as steel as a root that holds in the sea as she
  leans,
Leaning and laughing, my warm-hearted beauty, you ride,
  you ride,
You tack on the curves with parabola speed and a kiss of
  goodbye,
Like a thoroughbred sloop, my new high-spirited spirit, my
  kiss.

As my foot suggests that you leap in the air with your hips
  of a girl,
My finger that praises your wheel and announces your
  voices of song,
Flouncing your skirts, you blueness of joy, you flirt of
  politeness,
You leap, you intelligence, essence of wheelness with silvery
  nose,
And your platinum clocks of excitement stir like the hairs of
  a fern.

But how alien you are from the booming belts of your birth
  and the smoke
Where you turned on the stinging lathes of Detroit and
  Lansing at night
And shrieked at the torch in your secret parts and the
  amorous tests,
But now with your eyes that enter the future of roads you
  forget;
You are all instinct with your phosphorous glow and your
  streaking hair.

And now when we stop it is not as the bird from the shell
  that I leave
Or the leathery pilot who steps from his bird with a sneer of
  delight,

And not as the ignorant beast do you squat and watch me
　　depart,
But with exquisite breathing you smile, with satisfaction of
　　love,
And I touch you again as you tick in the silence and settle in
　　sleep.

My Grandmother

My grandmother moves to my mind in context of sorrow
And, as if apprehensive of near death, in black;
Whether erect in chair, her dry and corded throat harangued
    by grief,
Or at ragged book bent in Hebrew prayer,
Or gentle, submissive, and in tears to strangers;
Whether in sunny parlor or back of drawn blinds.

Though time and tongue made any love disparate,
On daguerreotype with classic perspective
Beauty I sigh and soften at is hers.
I pity her life of deaths, the agony of her own,
But most that history moved her through
Stranger lands and many houses,
Taking her exile for granted, confusing
The tongues and tasks of her children's children.

Necropolis

Even in death they prosper; even in the death
Where lust lies senseless and pride fallow
The mouldering owners of rents and labor
Prosper and improve the high hill.

For theirs is the stone whose name is deepest cut,
Theirs the facsimile temple, theirs
The iron acanthus and the hackneyed Latin,
The boxwood rows and all the birds.

And even in death the poor are thickly herded
In intimate congestion under streets and alleys.
Look at the standard sculpture, the cheap
Synonymous slabs, the machined crosses.

Yes, even in death the cities are unplanned.
The heirs govern from the old centers;
They will not remove. And the ludicrous angels,
Remains of the poor, will never fly
But only multiply in the green grass.

Scyros

snuffle and sniff and handkerchief

The doctor punched my vein
The captain called me Cain
Upon my belly sat the sow of fear
   With coins on either eye
   The President came by
And whispered to the braid what none could hear

High over where the storm
Stood steadfast cruciform
The golden eagle sank in wounded wheels
   White Negroes laughing still
   Crept fiercely on Brazil
Turning the navies upward on their keels

Now one by one the trees
Stripped to their naked knees
To dance upon the heaps of shrunken dead
   The roof of England fell
   Great Paris tolled her bell
And China staunched her milk and wept for bread

No island singly lay
But lost its name that day
The Ainu dived across the plunging sands
   From dawn to dawn to dawn
   King George's birds came on
Strafing the tulips from his children's hands

Thus in the classic sea
Southeast from Thessaly
The dynamited mermen washed ashore
   And tritons dressed in steel
   Trolled heads with rod and reel
And dredged potatoes from the Aegean floor

Hot is the sky and green
  Where Germans have been seen
The moon leaks metal on the Atlantic fields
  Pink boys in birthday shrouds
  Loop lightly through the clouds
Or coast the peaks of Finland on their shields

  That prophet year by year
  Lay still but could not hear
Where scholars tapped to find his new remains
  Gog and Magog ate pork
  In vertical New York
And war began next Wednesday on the Danes

Poet

Il arrive que l'esprit demande la poesie

Left leg flung out, head cocked to the right,
Tweed coat or army uniform, with book,
Beautiful eyes, who is this walking down?
Who, glancing at the pane of glass looks sharp
And thinks it is not he—as when a poet
Comes swiftly on some half-forgotten poem
And loosely holds the page, steady of mind,
        Thinking it is not his?

And when will *you* exist?—Oh, it is I,
Incredibly skinny, stooped, and neat as pie,
Ignorant as dirt, erotic as an ape,
Dreamy as puberty—with dirty hair!
Into the room like kangaroo he bounds,
Ears flopping like the most expensive hound's;
His chin receives all questions as he bows
        Mouthing a green bon-bon.

Has no more memory than rubber. Stands
Waist-deep in heavy mud of thought and broods
At his own wetness. When he would get out,
To his surprise he lifts in air a phrase
As whole and clean and silvery as a fish
Which jumps and dangles on his damned hooked grin,
But like a name-card on a man's label
        Calls him a conscious fool.

And child-like he remembers all his life
And cannily constructs it, fact by fact,
As boys paste postage stamps in careful books,
Denoting pence and legends and profiles,
Nothing more valuable.—And like a thief,
His eyes glassed over and congealed with guilt,
Fondles his secrets like a case of tools,
        And waits in empty doors.

By men despised for knowing what he is,
And by himself. But he exists for women.
As dolls to girls, as perfect wives to men,
So he to women. And to himself a thing,
All ages, epicene, without a trade.
To girls and wives always alive and fated;
To men and scholars always dead like Greek
        And always mistranslated.

Towards exile and towards shame he lures himself,
Tongue winding on his arm, and thinks like Eve
By biting apple will become most wise.
Sentio ergo sum: he feels his way
And words themselves stand up for him like Braille
And punch and perforate his parchment ear.
All language falls like Chinese on his soul,
        Image of song unsounded.

This is the coward's coward that in his dreams
Sees shapes of pain grow tall. Awake at night
He peers at sounds and stumbles at a breeze.
And none holds life less dear. For as a youth
Who by some accident observes his love
Naked and in some natural ugly act,
He turns with loathing and with flaming hands,
    Seared and betrayed by sight.

He is the business man, on beauty trades,
Dealer in arts and thoughts who, like the Jew,
Shall rise from slums and hated dialects
A tower of bitterness. Shall be always strange,
Hunted and then sought after. Shall be sat
Like an ambassador from another race
At tables rich with music. He shall eat flowers,
Chew honey and spit out gall. They shall all smile
        And love and pity him.

His death shall be by drowning. In that hour
When the last bubble of pure heaven's air

Hovers within his throat, safe on his bed,
A small eternal figurehead in terror,
He shall cry out and clutch his days of straw
Before the blackest wave. Lastly, his tomb
Shall list and founder in the troughs of grass
        And none shall speak his name.

Travelogue for Exiles

Look and remember. Look upon this sky;
Look deep and deep into the sea-clean air,
The unconfined, the terminus of prayer.
Speak now and speak into the hallowed dome.
What do you hear? What does the sky reply?
The heavens are taken: this is not your home.

Look and remember. Look upon this sea;
Look down and down into the tireless tide.
What of a life below, a life inside,
A tomb, a cradle in the curly foam?
The waves arise; sea-wind and sea agree
The waters are taken: this is not your home.

Look and remember. Look upon this land,
Far, far across the factories and the grass.
Surely, there, surely, they will let you pass.
Speak then and ask the forest and the loam.
What do you hear? What does the land command?
The earth is taken: this is not your home.

The Twins

Likeness has made them animal and shy.
See how they turn their full gaze left and right,
Seeking the other, yet not moving close;
Nothing in their relationship is gross,
But soft, conspicuous, like giraffes. And why
Do they not speak except by sudden sight?

Sisters kiss freely and unsubtle friends
Wrestle like lovers; brothers loudly laugh:
These in dreamier bondage dare not touch.
Each is the other's soul and hears too much
The heartbeat of the other; each apprehends
The sad duality and the imperfect half.

The one lay sick, the other wandered free,
But like a child to a small plot confined
Walked a short way and dumbly reappeared.
Is it not all-in-all of what they feared,
The single death, the obvious destiny
That maims the miracle their will designed?

For they go emptily from face to face,
Keeping the instinctive partnership of birth
A ponderous marriage and a sacred name;
Theirs is the price of shouldering each the same
The old indignity of Esau's race
And Dromio's denouement of tragic mirth.

Giantess

When Nature once in lustful hot undress
Conceived gargantuan offspring, then would I
Have loved to live near a young giantess,
Like a voluptuous cat at a queen's feet.

To see her body flower with her desire
And freely spread out in its dreadful play,
Guess if her heart concealed some heavy fire
Whose humid smokes would swim upon her eye;

To feel at leisure her stupendous shapes,
Crawl on the cliffs of her enormous knees,
And, when the unhealthy summer suns fatigued,

Have her stretch out across the plains and so
Sleep in the shadows of her breasts at ease
Like a small hamlet at a mountain's base.

(Baudelaire translation)

A Cut Flower

I stand on slenderness all fresh and fair,
I feel root-firmness in the earth far down,
I catch in the wind and loose my scent for bees
That sack my throat for kisses and suck love.
What is the wind that brings thy body over?
Wind, I am beautiful and sick. I long
For rain that strikes and bites like cold and hurts.
Be angry, rain, for dew is kind to me
When I am cool from sleep and take my bath.

Who softens the sweet earth about my feet,
Touches my face so often and brings water?
Where does she go, taller than any sunflower
Over the grass like birds? Has she a root?
These are great animals that kneel to us,
Sent by the sun perhaps to help us grow.
I have seen death. The colors went away,
The petals grasped at nothing and curled tight.
Then the whole head fell off and left the sky.

She tended me and held my by my stalk.
Yesterday I was well, and then the gleam,
The thing sharper than frost cut me in half.
I fainted and was lifted high. I feel
Waist-deep in rain. My face is dry and drawn.
My beauty leaks into the glass like rain.
When first I opened to the sun I thought
My colors would be parched. Where are my bees?
Must I die now? Is this a part of life?

Nigger

And did ever a man go black with sun in a Belgian swamp,
On a feathery African plain where the sunburnt lioness lies,
And a cocoanut monkey grove where the cockatoos scratch
the skies,
And the zebras striped with moonlight grasses gaze and
stomp?

With a swatch of the baboon's crimson bottom cut for a lip,
And a brace of elephant ivories hung for a tusky smile,
With the muscles as level and lazy and long as the lifting
Nile,
And a penis as loaded and supple and limp as the slaver's
whip?

Are you beautiful still when you walk downtown in a knife-
cut coat
And your yellow shoes dance at the corner curb like a brand
new car,
And the buck with the arching pick looks over the new-laid
tar
As you cock your eye like a cuckoo bird on a two-o'clock
note?

When you got so little in steel-rim specs, when you taught
that French,
When you wrote that book and you made that speech in the
bottom south,
When you beat that fiddle and sang that role for Othello's
mouth,
When you blew that horn for the shirt-sleeve mob and the
snaky wench?

When you boxed that hun, when you raped that trash that
you didn't rape,
When you caught that slug with a belly of fire and a face of
gray,
When you felt that loop and you took that boot from a
KKK,

And your hands hung down and your face went out in a
blast of grape?

Did the Lord say yes, did the Lord say no, did you ask the
Lord
When the jaw came down, when the cotton blossomed out
of your bones?
Are you coming to peace, O Booker T. Lincoln Roosevelt
Jones,
And is Jesus riding to raise your wage and to cut that cord?

The Synagogue

The synagogue dispirits the deep street,
Shadows the face of the pedestrian,
It is the adumbration of the Wall,
The stone survival that laments itself,
Our old entelechy of stubborn God,
Our calendar that marks a separate race.

The swift cathedral palpitates the blood,
The soul moves upward like a wing to meet
The pinnacles of saints. There flocks of thanks
In nooks of holy tracery arrive
And rested take their message in mid-air
Sphere after sphere into the papal heaven.

The altar of the Hebrews is a house,
No relic but a place, Sinai itself,
Not holy ground but factual holiness
Wherein the living god is resident.
Our scrolls are volumes of the thundered law
Sabbath by sabbath wound by hand to read.

He knows Al-Eloah to whom the Arab
Barefooted falls on sands, on table roofs,
In latticed alleys underneath the egg
On wide mosaics, when the crier shrills.
O profitable curse, most sacred rug,
Your book is blindness and your sword is rust.

And Judenhetze is the course of time;
We were rebellious, all but Abraham,
And skulked like Jonah, angry at the gourd.
Our days are captives in the minds of kings,
We stand in tens disjointed on the world
Grieving the ribbon of a coast we hated.

Some choose the ethics of belief beyond
Even particular election. Some
In bland memorial churches modify
The architecture of the state, and heaven

Disfranchised watches, caput mortuum,
The human substance eating, voting, smiling.

The Jew has no bedecked magnificat
But sits in stricken ashes after death,
Refusing grace; his grave is flowerless,
He gutters in the tallow of his name.
At Rome the multiplying tapers sing
Life endless in the history of art.

And Zion womanless refuses grace
To the first woman as to Magdalene,
But half-remembers Judith or Rahab,
The shrewd good heart of Esther honors still,
And weeps for almost sacred Ruth, but doubts
Either full harlotry or the faultless birth.

Our wine is wine, our bread is harvest bread
That feeds the body and is not the body.
Our blessing is to wine but not the blood
Nor to sangreal the sacred dish. We bless
The whiteness of the dish and bless the water
And are not anthropophagous to Him.

The immanent son then came as one of us
And stood against the ark. We have no prophets,
Our scholars are afraid. There have been friars,
Great healers, poets. The stars were terrible.
At the Sadducee court he touched our panic;
We were betrayed to sacrifice this man.

We live by virtue of philosophy,
Past love, and have our devious reward.
For faith He gave us land and took the land,
Making us exiles of all humankind.
Our name is yet the identity of God
That storms the falling altar of the world.

The Leg

Among the iodoform, in twilight-sleep,
What have I lost? he first inquires,
Peers in the middle distance where a pain,
Ghost of a nurse, hazily moves, and day,
Her blinding presence pressing in his eyes
And now his ears. They are handling him
With rubber hands. He wants to get up.

One day beside some flowers near his nose
He will be thinking, *When will I look at it?*
And pain, still in the middle distance, will reply,
At what? and he will know it's gone,
O where! and begin to tremble and cry.
He will begin to cry as a child cries
Whose puppy is mangled under a screaming wheel.

Later, as if deliberately, his fingers
Begin to explore the stump. He learns a shape
That is comfortable and tucked in like a sock.
This has a sense of humor, this can despise
The finest surgical limb, the dignity of limping,
The nonsense of wheel-chairs. Now he smiles to the wall:
The amputation becomes an acquisition.

For the leg is wondering where he is (all is not lost)
And surely he has a duty to the leg;
He is its injury, the leg is his orphan,
He must cultivate the mind of the leg,
Pray for the part that is missing, pray for peace
In the image of man, pray, pray for its safety,
And after a little it will die quietly.

The body, what is it, Father, but a sign
To love the force that grows us, to give back
What in Thy palm is senselessness and mud?
Knead, knead the substance of our understanding
Which must be beautiful in flesh to walk,
That if Thou take me angrily in hand
And hurl me to the shark, I shall not die!

The Interlude

I

Much of transfiguration that we hear,
The ballet of the atoms, the second law
Of thermo-dynamics, Isis, and the queer

Fertilization of fish, the Catholic's awe
For the life-cycle of the Nazarene,
His wife whom sleeping Milton thought he saw;

Much of the resurrection that we've seen
And taken part in, like the Passion Play,
All of autumnal red and April green,

To those who walk in work from day to day,
To economic and responsible man,
All, all is substance. Life that lets him stay

Uses his substance kindly while she can
But drops him lifeless after his one span.

II

What lives? the proper creatures in their homes?
A weed? the white and giddy butterfly?
Bacteria? necklaces of chromosomes?

What lives: the breathing bell of the clear sky?
The crazed bull of the sea? Andean crags?
Armies that plunge into themselves to die?

People? A sacred relic wrapped in rags,
The ham-bone of a saint, the winter rose,
Do these?—And is there not a hand that drags

The bottom of the universe for those
Who still perhaps are breathing? Listen well,
There lives a quiet like a cathedral close

At the soul's center where substance cannot dwell
And life flowers like music from a bell.

III

Writing, I crushed an insect with my nail
And thought nothing at all. A bit of wing
Caught my eye then, a gossamer so frail

And exquisite, I saw in it a thing
That scorned the grossness of the thing I wrote.
It hung upon my finger like a sting.

A leg I noticed next, fine as a mote,
"And on this frail eyelash he walked," I said,
"And climbed and walked like any mountain-goat."

And in this mood I sought the little head,
But it was lost; then in my heart a fear
Cried out, "A life—why beautiful, why dead!"

It was a mite that held itself most dear,
So small I could have drowned it with a tear.

The Intellectual

What should the wars do with these jigging fools?

The man behind the book may not be man,
His own man or the book's or yet the time's,
But still be whole, deciding what he can
In praise of politics or German rimes;

But the intellectual lights a cigarette
And offers it lit to the lady, whose odd smile
Is the merest hyphen—lest he should forget
What he has been resuming all the while.

He talks to overhear, she to withdraw
To some interior feminine fireside
Where the back arches, beauty puts forth a paw
Like a black puma stretching in velvet pride,

Making him think of cats, a stray of which
Some days sets up a howling in his brain,
Pure interference such as this neat bitch
Seems to create from listening disdain.

But talk is all the value, the release,
Talk is the very fillip of an act,
The frame and subject of the masterpiece
Under whose film of age the face is cracked.

His own forehead glows like expensive wood,
But back of it the mind is disengaged,
Self-sealing clock recording bad and good
At constant temperature, intact, unaged.

But strange, his body is an open house
Inviting every passerby to stay;
The city to and fro beneath his brows
Wanders and drinks and chats from night to day.

Think of a private thought, indecent room
Where one might kiss his daughter before bed!

Life is embarrassed; shut the family tomb,
Console your neighbor for his recent dead;

Do something! die in Spain or paint a green
Gouache, go into business (Rimbaud did),
Or start another Little Magazine,
Or move in with a woman, have a kid.

Invulnerable, impossible, immune,
Do what you will, your will will not be done
But dissipate the light of afternoon
Till evening flickers like the midnight sun,

And midnight shouts and dies: I'd rather be
A milkman walking in his sleep at dawn
Bearing fat quarts of cream, and so be free,
Crossing alone and cold from lawn to lawn.

I'd rather be a barber and cut hair
Than walk with you in gilt museum halls,
You and the puma-lady, she so rare
Exhaling her silk soul upon the walls.

Go take yourselves apart, but let me be
The fault you find with everyman. I spit,
I laugh, I fight; and you, *l'homme qui rît*,
Swallow your stale saliva, and still sit.

V-Letter

I love you first because your face is fair,
        Because your eyes Jewish and blue,
Set sweetly with the touch of foreignness
Above the cheekbones, stare rather than dream.
Often your countenance recalls a boy
        Blue-eyed and small, whose silent mischief
Tortured his parents and compelled my hate
        To wish his ugly death.
Because of this reminder, my soul's trouble,
And for your face, so often beautiful,
        I love you, wish you life.

I love you first because you wait, because
        For your own sake, I cannot write
Beyond these words. I love you for these words
That sting and creep like insects and leave filth.
I love you for the poverty you cry
        And I bend down with tears of steel
That melt your hand like wax, not for this war
        The droplets shattering
Those candle-glowing fingers of my joy,
But for your name of agony, my love,
        That cakes my mouth with salt.

And all your imperfections and perfections
        And all your magnitude of grace
And all this love explained and unexplained
Is just a breath. I see you woman-size
And this looms larger and more goddess-like
        Than silver goddesses on screens.
I see you in the ugliness of light,
        Yet you are beautiful,
And in the dark of absence your full length
Is such as meets my body to the full
        Though I am starved and huge.

You turn me from these days as from a scene
        Out of an open window far

Where lies the foreign city and the war.
You are my home and in your spacious love
I dream to march as under flaring flags
          Until the door is gently shut.
Give me the tearless lesson of your pride,
          Teach me to live and die
As one deserving anonymity,
The mere devotion of a house to keep
          A woman and a man.

Give me the free and poor inheritance
          Of our own kind, not furniture
Of education, nor the prophet's pose,
The general cause of words, the hero's stance,
The ambitions incommensurable with flesh,
          But the drab makings of a room
Where sometimes in the afternoon of thought
          The brief and blinding flash
May light the enormous chambers of your will
And show the gracious Parthenon that time
          Is ever measured by.

As groceries in pantry gleam and smile
          Because they are important weights
Bought with the metal minutes of your pay,
So do these hours stand in solid rows,
The dowry for a use in common life.
          I love you first because your years
Lead to my matter-of-fact and simple death
          Or to our open marriage,
And I pray nothing for my safety back,
Not even luck, because our love is whole
          Whether I live or fail.

The Conscientious Objector

The gates clanged and they walked you into jail
More tense than felons but relieved to find
The hostile world shut out, the flags that dripped
From every mother's windowpane, obscene
The bloodlust sweating from the public heart,
The dog authority slavering at your throat.
A sense of quiet, of pulling down the blind
Possessed you. Punishment you felt was clean.

The decks, the catwalks, and the narrow light
Composed a ship. This was a mutinous crew
Troubling the captains for plain decencies,
A Mayflower brim with pilgrims headed out
To establish new theocracies to west,
A Noah's ark coasting the topmost seas
Ten miles above the sodomites and fish.
These inmates loved the only living doves.

Like all men hunted from the world you made
A good community, voyaging the storm
To no safe Plymouth or green Ararat;
Trouble or calm, the men with Bibles prayed,
The gaunt politicals construed our hate.
The opposite of all armies, you were best
Opposing uniformity and yourselves;
Prison and personality were your fate.

You suffered not so physically but knew
Maltreatment, hunger, ennui of the mind.
Well might the soldier kissing the hot beach
Erupting in his face damn all your kind.
Yet you who saved neither yourselves nor us
Are equally with those who shed the blood
The heroes of our cause. Your conscience is
What we come back to in the armistice.

The Progress of Faust

He was born in Deutschland, as you would suspect,
And graduated in magic from Cracow
In Fifteen Five. His portraits show a brow
Heightened by science. The eye is indirect,
As of bent light upon a crooked soul,
And that he bargained with the Prince of Shame
For pleasures intellectually foul
Is known by every court that lists his name.

His frequent disappearances are put down
To visits in the regions of the damned
And to the periodic deaths he shammed,
But, unregenerate and in Doctor's gown,
He would turn up to lecture at the fair
And do a minor miracle for a fee.
Many a life he whispered up the stair
To teach the black art of anatomy.

He was as deaf to angels as an oak
When, in the fall of Fifteen Ninety-four,
He went to London and crashed through the floor
In mock damnation of the playgoing folk.
Weekending with the scientific crowd,
He met Sir Francis Bacon and helped draft
"Colours of Good and Evil" and read aloud
An obscene sermon at which no one laughed.

He toured the Continent for a hundred years
And subsidized among the peasantry
The puppet play, his tragic history;
With a white glove he boxed the devil's ears
And with a black his own. Tired of this,
He published penny poems about his sins,
In which he placed the heavy emphasis
On the white glove which, for a penny, wins.

Some time before the hemorrhage of the Kings
Of France, he turned respectable and taught;

Quite suddenly everything that he had thought
Seemed to grow scholars' beards and angels' wings.
It was the Overthrow. On Reason's throne
He sat with the fair Phrygian on his knees
And called all universities his own,
As plausible a figure as you please.

Then back to Germany as the sages' sage
To preach comparative science to the young
Who came from every land in a great throng
And knew they heard the master of the age.
When for a secret formula he paid
The Devil another fragment of his soul,
His scholars wept, and several even prayed
That Satan would restore him to them whole.

Backwardly tolerant, Faustus was expelled
From the Third Reich in Nineteen Thirty-nine.
His exit caused the breaching of the Rhine,
Except for which the frontier might have held.
Five years unknown to enemy and friend
He hid, appearing on the sixth to pose
In an American desert at war's end
Where, at his back, a dome of atoms rose.

Boy-Man

England's lads are miniature men
To start with, grammar in their shiny hats,
And serious: in America who knows when
Manhood begins? Presidents dance and hug
And while the kind King waves and gravely chats
America wets on England's old green rug.

The boy-man roars. Worry alone will give
This one the verisimilitude of age.
Those white teeth are his own, for he must live
Longer, grow taller than the Texas race.
Fresh are his eyes, his darkening skin the gauge
Of bloods that freely mix beneath his face.

He knows the application of the book
But not who wrote it; shuts it like a shot.
Rather than read he thinks that he will look,
Rather than look he thinks that he will talk,
Rather than talk he thinks that he will not
Bother at all; would rather ride than walk.

His means of conversation is the joke,
Humor his language underneath which lies
The undecoded dialect of the folk.
Abroad he scorns the foreigner: what's old
Is worn, what's different bad, what's odd unwise.
He gives off heat and is enraged by cold.

Charming, becoming to the suits he wears,
The boy-man, younger than his eldest son,
Inherits the state; upon his silver hairs
Time like a panama hat sits at a tilt
And smiles. To him the world has just begun
And every city waiting to be built.

Mister, remove your shoulder from the wheel
And say this prayer, "Increase my vitamins,
Make my decisions of the finest steel,

Pour motor oil upon my troubled spawn,
Forgive the Europeans for their sins,
Establish them, that values may go on."

The New Ring

The new ring oppresses the finger, embarrasses the hand, encumbers the whole arm. The free hand moves to cover the new ring, except late-at-night when the mouth reaches to kiss the soft silver, a sudden thought.

In the lodge of marriage, the secret society of love, the perfect circle binds and separates, moves and is stationary.

Till the ring becomes the flesh, leaving a white trench, and the finger is immune. For the brand is assumed. Till the flesh of the encumbered hand grows over the ring, as living wood over and around the iron spike. Till the value of the reason of the gift is coinworn, and the wound heals.

And until the wound heals, the new ring is a new nail driven through the hand upon the living wood, the body hangs from the nail, and the nail holds.

The Dirty Word

The dirty word hops in the cage of the mind like the Pondi-cherry vulture, stomping with its heavy left claw on the sweet meat of the brain and tearing it with its vicious beak, ripping and chopping the flesh. Terrified, the small boy bears the big bird of the dirty word into the house, and grunting, puffing, carries it up the stairs to his own room in the skull. Bits of black feather cling to his clothes and his hair as he locks the staring creature in the dark closet.

All day the small boy returns to the closet to examine and feed the bird, to caress and kick the bird, that now snaps and flaps its wings savagely whenever the door is opened. How the boy trembles and delights at the sight of the white excre-ment of the bird! How the bird leaps and rushes against the walls of the skull, trying to escape from the zoo of the vocabu-lary! How wildly snaps the sweet meat of the brain in its rage.

And the bird outlives the man, being freed at the man's death-funeral by a word from the rabbi.

But I one morning went upstairs and opened the door and entered the closet and found in the cage of my mind the great bird dead. Softly I wept it and softly removed it and softly buried the body of the bird in the hollyhock garden of the house I lived in twenty years before. And out of the worn black feathers of the wing have I made pens to write these elegies, for I have outlived the bird, and I have murdered it in my early manhood.

Adam and Eve

I   The Sickness of Adam

In the beginning, at every step, he turned
As if by instinct to the East to praise
The nature of things. Now every path was learned
He lost the lifted, almost flower-like gaze

Of a temple dancer. He began to walk
Slowly, like one accustomed to be alone.
He found himself lost in the field of talk;
Thinking became a garden of its own.

In it were new things: words he had never said,
Beasts he had never seen and knew were not
In the true garden, terrors, and tears shed
Under a tree by him, for some new thought.

And the first anger. Once he flung a staff
At softly coupling sheep and struck the ram.
It broke away. And God heard Adam laugh
And for his laughter made the creature lame.

And wanderlust. He stood upon the Wall
To search the unfinished countries lying wide
And waste, where not a living thing could crawl,
And yet he would descend, as if to hide.

His thought drew down the guardian at the gate,
To whom man said, "What danger am I in?"
And the angel, hurt in spirit, seemed to hate
The wingless thing that worried after sin,

For it said nothing but marvelously unfurled
Its wings and arched them shimmering overhead,
Which must have been the signal from the world
That the first season of our life was dead.

Adam fell down with labor in his bones,
And God approached him in the cool of day
And said, "This sickness in your skeleton
Is longing. I will remove if from your clay."

He said also, "I made you strike the sheep."
It began to rain and God sat down beside
The sinking man. When he was fast asleep
He wet his right hand deep in Adam's side

And drew the graceful rib out of his breast.
Far off, the latent streams began to flow
And birds flew out of Paradise to nest
On earth. Sadly the angel watched them go.

II   The Recognition of Eve

Whatever it was she had so fiercely fought
Had fled back to the sky, but still she lay
With arms outspread, awaiting its assault,
Staring up through the branches of the tree,
The fig tree. Then she drew a shuddering breath
And turned her head instinctively his way.
She had fought birth as dying men fight death.

Her sigh awakened him. He turned and saw
A body swollen, as though formed of fruits,
White as the flesh of fishes, soft and raw.
He hoped she was another of the brutes
So he crawled over and looked into her eyes,
The human wells that pool all absolutes.
It was like looking into double skies.

And when she spoke the first word (it was *thou*)
He was terror-stricken, but she raised her hand
And touched his wound where it was fading now,
For he must feel the place to understand.
Then he recalled the longing that had torn

His side, and while he watched it whitely mend,
He felt it stab him suddenly like a thorn.

He thought the woman had hurt him. Was it she
Or the same sickness seeking to return;
Or was there any difference, the pain set free
And she who seized him now as hard as iron?
Her fingers bit his body. She looked old
And involuted, like the newly-born.
He let her hurt him till she loosed her hold.

Then she forgot him and she wearily stood
And went in search of water through the grove.
Adam could see her wandering through the wood,
Studying her footsteps as her body wove
In light and out of light. She found a pool
And there he followed shyly to observe.
She was already turning beautiful.

III   The Kiss

The first kiss was with stumbling fingertips.
Their bodies grazed each other as if by chance
And touched and untouched in a kind of dance.
Second, they found out touching with their lips.

Some obscure angel, pausing on his course,
Shed such a brightness on the face of Eve
That Adam in grief was ready to believe
He had lost her love. The third kiss was by force.

Their lips formed foreign, unimagined oaths
When speaking of the Tree of Guilt. So wide
Their mouths, they drank each other from inside.
A gland of honey burst within their throats.

But something rustling hideously overhead,
They jumped up from the fourth caress and hid.

IV   The Tree of Guilt

Why, on her way to the oracle of Love,
Did she not even glance up at the Tree
Of Life, that giant with whitish cast
And glinting leaves and berries of dull gray,
As though covered with mold? But who would taste
The medicine of immortality,
And who would "be as God?" And in what way?

So she came breathless to the lowlier one
And like a priestess of the cult she knelt,
Holding her breasts in token for a sign,
And prayed the spirit of the burdened bough
That the great power of the tree be seen
And lift itself out of the Tree of Guilt
Where it had hidden in the leaves till now.

Or did she know already? Had the peacock
Rattling its quills, glancing its thousands eyes
At her, the iridescence of the dove,
Stench of the he-goat, everything that joins
Told her the mystery? It was not enough,
So from the tree the snake began to rise
And dropt its head and pointed at her loins.

She fell and hid her face and still she saw
The spirit of the tree emerge and slip
Into the open sky until it stood
Straight as a standing-stone, and spilled its seed.
And all the seed were serpents of the good.
Again the snake was seized and from its lip
It spat the venomous evil of the deed.

And it was over. But the woman lay
Stricken with what she knew, ripe in her thought
Like a fresh apple fallen from the limb
And rotten, like a fruit that lies too long.
This way she rose, ripe-rotten in her prime

And spurned the cold thing coiled against her foot
And called her husband, in a kind of song.

V   The Confession

As on the first day her first word was *thou*.
He waited while she said, "Thou art the tree."
And while she said, almost accusingly,
Looking at nothing, "Thou are the fruit I took"
She seemed smaller by inches as she spoke,
And Adam wondering touched her hair and shook,
Half understanding. He answered softly, "How?"

And for the third time, in the third way, Eve:
"The tree that rises from the middle part
Of the garden." And almost tenderly, "Thou art
The garden. *We.*" Then she was overcome,
And Adam coldly, lest he should succumb
To pity, standing at the edge of doom,
Comforted her like one about to leave.

She sensed departure and she stood aside
Smiling and bitter. But he asked again,
"How did you eat? With what thing did you sin?"
And Eve with body slackened and uncouth,
"Under the tree I took the fruit of truth
From an angel. I ate it with my other mouth."
And saying so, she did not know she lied.

It was the man who suddenly released
From doubt, wept in the woman's heavy arms,
Those double serpents, subtly winding forms
That climb and drop about the manly boughs,
And dry with weeping, fiery and aroused,
Fell on her face to slake his terrible thirst
And bore her body earthward like a beast.

VI Shame

The hard blood falls back in the manly fount,
The soft door closes under Venus' mount,
The ovoid moon moves to the Garden's side
And dawn comes, but the lovers have not died.
They have not died but they have fallen apart.
In sleep, like equal halves of the same heart.

How to teach shame? How to teach nakedness
To the already naked? How to express
Nudity? How to open innocent eyes
And separate the innocent from the wise?
And how to re-establish the guilty tree
In infinite gardens of humanity?

By marring the image, by the black device
Of the goat-god, by the clown of Paradise,
By fruits of cloth and by the navel's bud,
By itching tendrils and by strings of blood,
By ugliness, by the shadow of our fear,
By ridicule, by the fig-leaf patch of hair.

Whiter than tombs, whiter than whitest clay,
Exposed beneath the whitening eye of day,
They awoke and saw the covering that reveals.
They thought they were changing into animals.
Like animals they bellowed terrible cries
And clutched each other, hiding each other's eyes.

VII Exile

The one who gave the warning with his wings,
Still doubting them, held out the sword of flame
Against the Tree of Whiteness as they came
Angrily, slowly by, like exiled kings,

And watched them at the broken-open gate
Stare in the distance long and overlong,
And then, like peasants, pitiful and strong,
Take the first step toward earth and hesitate.

For Adam raised his head and called aloud,
"My Father, who has made the garden pall,
Giving me all things and then taking all,
Who with your opposite nature has endowed

Woman, give us your hand for our descent.
Needing us greatly, even in our disgrace,
Guide us, for gladly do we leave this place
For our own land and wished-for banishment."

But woman prayed, "Guide us to Paradise."
Around them slunk the uneasy animals,
Strangely excited, uttering coughs and growls,
And bounded down into the wild abyss.

And overhead the last migrating birds,
Then empty sky. And when the two had gone
A slow half-dozen steps across the stone,
The angel came and stood among the shards

And called them, as though joyously, by name.
They turned in dark amazement and beheld
Eden ablaze with fires of red and gold,
The garden dressed for dying in cold flame,

And it was autumn, and the present world.

Israel

When I think of the liberation of Palestine,
When my eye conceives the great black English line
Spanning the world news of two thousand years,
My heart leaps forward like a hungry dog,
My heart is thrown back on its tangled chain,
My soul is hangdog in a Western chair.

When I think of the battle for Zion I hear
The drop of chains, the starting forth of feet
And I remain chained in a Western chair.
My blood beats like a bird against a wall,
I feel the weight of prisons in my skull
Falling away; my forebears stare through stone.

When I see the name of Israel high in print
The fences crumble in my flesh; I sink
Deep in a Western chair and rest my soul.
I look the stranger clear to the blue depths
Of his unclouded eye. I say my name
Aloud for the first time unconsciously.

Speak of the tillage of a million heads
No more. Speak of the evil myth no more
Of one who harried Jesus on his way
Saying, *Go faster*. Speak no more
Of the yellow badge, *secta nefaria*.
Speak the name only of the living land.

Glass Poem

The afternoon lies glazed upon the wall
And on the window shines the scene-like bay,
And on the dark reflective floor a ray
Falls, and my thoughts like ashes softly fall.

And I look up as one who looks through glass
And sees the thing his soul clearly desires,
Who stares until his vision flags and tires,
But from whose eye the image fails to pass;

Until a wish crashes the vitreous air
And comes to your real hands across this space,
Thief-like and deeply cut to touch your face,
Dearly, most bitterly to touch your hair.

And I could shatter these transparent lights,
Could thrust my arms and bring your body through,
Break from the subtle spectrum the last hue
And change my eyes to dark soft-seeing nights.

But the sun stands and the hours stare like brass
And day flows thickly into permanent time,
And toward your eyes my threatening wishes climb
Where you move through a sea of solid glass.

The Tingling Back

Sometimes deeply immured in white-washed tower
    quiet at ink and thinking book,
        alone with my own smoke,
the blood at rest, the body far below,
    swiftly there falls an angry shower
        of arrows upon my back,
like bees or electric needles run amok
    between my flesh and shirt. I know
        then I have touched the pain
of amour-propre, of something yesterday
    I said and I should not have said,
        I did and must not do.
These needles wing their insights from my brain
    and through and through my flesh they play
        to prick my skin with red
letters of shame and blue blurs of tattoo.
    I sweat and take my medicine
        for one must be sincere
and study one's sincerity like a crime:
    to be the very last to smile,
        the first one to begin
(when danger streaks the atmosphere) to fear,
    to pocket praises like a dime,
        to pet the crocodile,
to see a foreign agony as stone,
    to ravel dreams in crowded room,
        to let the hair grow tall,
to skin the eye and thrust it to the wind.
    Yet if I stood with God alone
        inside the blinding tomb
I would not feel embarrassment at all
    nor those hot needles of the mind
        which are so clean. I'd ask
not if I'd known the tissue of my will
    and scarified my body white,
        but whether, insincere,

I'd grown to the simplicity of a mask;
  and if in natural error still
      whether my fingers might
destroy the true and keep the error near.

Love for a Hand

Two hands lie still, the hairy and the white,
And soon down ladders of reflected light
The sleepers climb in silence. Gradually
They separate on paths of long ago,
Each winding on his arm the unpleasant clew
That leads, live as a nerve, to memory.

But often when too steep her dream descends,
Perhaps to the grotto where her father bends
To pick her up, the husband wakes as though
He had forgotten something in the house.
Motionless he eyes the room that glows
With the little animals of light that prowl

This way and that. Soft are the beasts of light
But softer still her hand that drifts so white
Upon the whiteness. How like a water-plant
It floats upon the black canal of sleep,
Suspended upward from the distant deep
In pure achievement of its lovely want!

Quietly then he plucks it and it folds
And is again a hand, small as a child's.
He would revive it but it barely stirs
And so he carries it off a little way
And breaks it open gently. Now he can see
The sweetness of the fruit, his hand eats hers.

The Figurehead

Watching my paralytic friend
Caught in the giant clam of himself
Fast on the treacherous shoals of his bed,
I look away to the place he had left
Where at a decade's distance he appeared
To pause in his walk and think of a limp.
One day he arrived at the street bearing
The news that he dragged an ancient foot:
The people on their porches seemed to sway.

Though there are many wired together
In this world and the next, my friend
Strains in his clamps. He is all sprung
And locked in the rust of inner change.
The therapist who plucks him like a harp
Is a cold torture: the animal bleats
And whimpers on its far seashore
As she leans to her find with a smooth hunger.

Somewhere in a storm my pity went down:
It was a wooden figurehead
With sea-hard breasts and polished mouth.
But women wash my friend with brine
From shallow inlets of their eyes,
And women rock my friend with waves
That pulsate from the female moon.
They gather at his very edge and haul
My driftwood friend toward their fires.

Speaking of dancing, joking of sex,
I watch my paralytic friend
And seek my pity in those wastes where he
Becomes my bobbing figurehead.
Then as I take my leave I wade
Loudly into the shallows of his pain,
I splash like a vacationer,
I scare his legs and stir the time of day
With rosy clouds of sediment.

A Calder

To raise an iron tree
Is a wooden irony,
But to cause it to sail
In a clean perpetual way
Is to play
Upon the spaces of the scale.
Climbing the stairs we say,
Is it work or is it play?

Alexander Calder made it
Work and play:
Leaves that will never burn
But were fired to be born,
Twigs that are stiff with life
And bend as to the magnet's breath,
Each segment back to back,
The whole a hanging burst of flak.

Still the base metals,
Touched by autumnal paint
Fall through no autumn
But, turning, feint
In a fall beyond trees,
Where forests are not wooded,
There is no killing breeze,
And iron is blooded.

The Alphabet

The letters of the Jews as strict as flames
Or little terrible flowers lean
Stubbornly upwards through the perfect ages,
Singing through solid stone the sacred names.
The letters of the Jews are black and clean
And lie in chain-line over Christian pages.
The chosen letters bristle like barbed wire
That hedge the flesh of man,
Twisting and tightening the book that warns.
These words, this burning bush, this flickering pyre
Unsacrifices the bled son of man
Yet plaits his crown of thorns.

Where go the tipsy idols of the Roman
Past synagogues of patient time,
Where go the sisters of the Gothic rose,
Where go the blue eyes of the Polish women
Past the almost natural crime,
Past the still speaking embers of ghettos,
There rise the tinder flowers of the Jews.
The letters of the Jews are dancing knives
That carve the heart of darkness seven ways.
These are the letters that all men refuse
And will refuse until the king arrives
And will refuse until the death of time
And all is rolled back in the book of days.

Messias

Alone in the darkling apartment the boy
Was reading poetry when the doorbell rang;
The sound sped to his ear and winged his joy,
The book leaped from his lap on broken wing.

Down the gilt stairwell then he peered
Where an old man of patriarchal race
Climbed in an eastern language with his beard
A black halo around his paper face.

His glasses spun with vision and his hat
Was thick with fur in the August afternoon;
His silk suit crackled heavily with light
And in his hand a rattling canister shone.

Bigger he grew and softer the root words
Of the hieratic language of his heart,
And faced the boy, who flung the entrance wide
And fled in terror from the nameless hurt.

Past every door like a dead thing he swam,
Past the entablatures of the kitchen walls,
Down the red ringing of the fire escape
Singing with sun, to the green grass he came,

Sickeningly green, leaving the man to lurch
Bewildered through the house and seat himself
In the sacrificial kitchen after his march,
To study the strange boxes on the shelf.

There mother found him mountainous and alone,
Mumbling some singsong in a monotone,
Crumbling breadcrumbs in his scholar's hand
That wanted a donation for the Holy Land.

The Olive Tree

Save for a lusterless honing-stone of moon
The sky stretches its flawless canopy
Blue as the blue silk of the Jewish flag
Over the valley and out to sea.
It is bluest just above the olive tree.
You cannot find in twisted Italy
So straight a one; it stands not on a crag,
Is not humpbacked with bearing in scored stone,
But perfectly erect in my front yard,
Oblivious of its fame. The fruit is hard,
Multitudinous, acid, tight on the stem;
The leaves ride boat-like in the brimming sun,
Going nowhere and scooping up the light.
It is the silver tree, the holy tree,
Tree of all attributes.
                              Now on the lawn
The olives fall by thousands, and I delight
To shed my tennis shoes and walk on them,
Pressing them coldly into the deep grass,
In love and reverence for the total loss.

The First Time

Behind shut doors, in shadowy quarantine,
There shines the lamp of iodine and rose
That stains all love with its medicinal bloom.
This boy, who is no more than seventeen,
Not knowing what to do, takes off his clothes
As one might in a doctor's anteroom.

Then in a cross-draft of fear and shame
Feels love hysterically burn away,
A candle swimming down to nothingness
Put out by its own wetted gusts of flame,
And he stands smooth as uncarved ivory
Heavily curved for some expert caress.

And finally sees the always open door
That is invisible till the time has come,
And half falls through as through a rotten wall
To where chairs twist with dragons from the floor
And the great bed drugged with its own perfume
Spreads its carnivorous flower-mouth for all.

The girl is sitting with her back to him;
She wears a black thing and she rakes her hair,
Hauling her round face upward like moonrise;
She is younger than he, her angled arms are slim
And like a country girl her feet are bare.
She watches him behind her with old eyes,

Transfixing him in space like some grotesque,
Far, far from her where he is still alone
And being here is more and more untrue.
Then she turns round, as one turns at a desk,
And looks at him, too naked and too soon,
And almost gently asks: *Are you a Jew?*

The Crucifix in the Filing Cabinet

Out of the filing cabinet of true steel
That saves from fire my rags of letters, bills,
Manuscripts, contracts, all the trash of praise
Which one acquires to prove and prove his days;

Out of the drawer that rolls on hidden wheels
I drew a crucifix with beaded chain,
Still new and frightened-looking and absurd.
I picked it up as one picks up a bird

And placed it on my palm. It formed a pile
Like a small mound of stones on which there stands
A tree crazy with age, and on the tree
Some ancient teacher hanging by his hands.

I found a velvet bag sewn by the Jews
For holy shawls and frontlets and soft thongs
That bind the arm at morning for great wrongs
Done in a Pharaoh's time. The crucifix

I dropped down in the darkness of this pouch,
Thought tangled with thought and chain with chain,
Till time untie the dark with greedy look,
Crumble the cross and bleed the leathery vein.

Solipsism

The world is my dream, says the wise child, ever so wise, not
stepping on lines. I am the world, says the wise-eyed
child. I made you, mother. I made you, sky. Take care
or I'll put you back in my dream.

If I look at the sun the sun will explode, says the wicked boy.
If I look at the moon I'll drain away. Where I stay I
hold them in their places. Don't ask me what I'm
doing.

The simple son was sent to science college. There he learned
how everything worked.

The one who says nothing is told everything (not that he
cares). The one who dreamed me hasn't put me back.
The sun and the moon, they rise on time. I still don't
know how the engine works; I can splice a wire. That's
about it.

The dream is my world, says the sick child. I am pure as these
bed sheets. (He writes fatigue on the vast expanses.)
I'm in your dream, says the wicked boy. The simple
son has been decorated for objectivity. He who says
nothing is still being told.

Office Love

Office love, love of money and fight, love of calculated sex. The offices reek with thin volcanic metal. Tears fall in typewriters like drops of solder. Brimstone of brassieres, low voices, the whirr of dead-serious play. From the tropical tree and the Rothko in the Board Room to the ungrammatical broom closet fragrant with waxes, to the vast typing pool where coffee is being served by dainty waitresses maneuvering their hand trucks, music almost unnoticeable falls. The very telephones are hard and kissable, the electric water cooler sweetly sweats. Gold simmers to a boil in braceleted and sunburned cheeks. What ritual politeness nevertheless, what subtlety of clothing. And if glances meet, if shoulders graze, there's no harm done. Flowers, celebrations, pregnancy leave, how the little diamonds sparkle under the psychologically soft-colored ceilings. It's an elegant windowless world of soft pressures and efficiency joys, of civilized mishaps—mere runs in the stocking, papercuts.

Where the big boys sit the language is rougher. Phone calls to China and a private shower. No paper visible anywhere. Policy is decided by word of mouth like gangsters. There the power lies and is sexless.

I Am an Atheist Who Says His Prayers

I am an atheist who says his prayers.

I am an anarchist, and a full professor at that. I take the loyalty oath.

I am a deviate. I fondle and contribute, backscuttle and brown, father of three.

I stand high in the community. My name is in *Who's Who*. People argue about my modesty.

I drink my share and yours and never have enough. I free-load officially and unofficially.

A physical coward, I take on all intellectuals, established poets, popes, rabbis, chiefs of staff.

I am a mystic. I will take an oath that I have seen the Virgin. Under the dry pandanus, to the scratching of kangaroo rats, I achieve psychic onanism. My tree of nerves electrocutes itself.

I uphold the image of America and force my luck. I write my own ticket to oblivion.

I am of the race wrecked by success. The audience brings me news of my death. I write out of boredom, despise solemnity. The wrong reason is good enough for me.

I am of the race of the prematurely desperate. In poverty of comfort I lay gunpowder plots. I lapse my insurance.

I am the Babbitt metal of the future. I never read more than half of a book. But that half I read forever.

I love the palimpsest, statues without heads, fertility dolls of the continent of Mu. I dream prehistory, the invention of dye. The palms of the dancers' hands are vermillion. Their heads oscillate like the cobra. High-caste woman smelling of earth and silk, you can dry my feet with your hair.

I take my place beside the Philistine and unfold my napkin. This afternoon I defend the Marines. I goggle at long cars.

Without compassion I attack the insane. Give them the horsewhip!

The homosexual lectures me brilliantly in the beer booth. I can feel my muscles soften. He smiles at my terror.

Pitchpots flicker in the lemon groves. I gaze down on the plains of Hollywood. My fine tan and my arrogance, my gray hair and my sneakers, O Israel!

Wherever I am I become. The power of entry is with me. In the doctor's office a patient, calm and humiliated. In the foreign movies a native, shabby enough. In the art gallery a person of authority (there's a secret way of approaching a picture. Others move off). The high official insults me to my face. I say nothing and accept the job. He offers me whiskey.

How beautifully I fake! I convince myself with men's room jokes and epigrams. I paint myself into a corner and escape on pulleys of the unknown. Whatever I think at the moment is true. Turn me around in my tracks; I will take your side.

For the rest, I improvise and am not spiteful and water the plants on the cocktail table.

Statue of Liberty

To the poor (aux pauvres) crime alone (le crime seul) opens
(ouvre les portes de la vie) the doors of life. Entire li-
braries of music are hurled in the gutters: the G.I.'s are
looking for bottles. The Bavarian Venus is snatched
baldheaded.

I have a big sister; she has mighty breasts. She writes poems
for the immigration office. Her crotch is on the four-
teenth floor. La géante, la géante!

Standing at the pure white rail, stately we pass you, and the
classes mingle as if by decree. At the last buoy the dis-
creet signs begin to take effect: First Class, Second
Class. My brazen sister swirling her nightgown, green
as the spouts of Chartres. Her comb is combing my lice
(but I have no lice). Her apron is hitched up in front.
She stands on a full-sized bank.

Across the iambic pentameter of the Atlantic (the pilot
dropped, the station wagon in the hold) we sail to the
kingdom of Small. Is it cheaper there? Can I buy a slave?

Nebraska

I love Nowhere where the factories die of malnutrition.

I love Nowhere where there are no roads, no rivers, no interesting Indians,

Where history is invented in the History Department and there are no centennials of anything,

Where every tree is planted by hand and has a private tutor.

Where the "parts" have to be ordered and the sky settles all questions,

Where travelers from California bitch at the backwardness and New Yorkers step on the gas in a panic,

Where the grass in winter is gray not brown,

Where the population diminishes.

Here on the boundary of the hired West, equidistant from every tourist office, and the air is washed by distance, here at last there is nothing to recommend.

May no one ever attempt a recommendation; Chicago be as far as Karachi.

Though the warriors come with rockets, may they fall off the trucks.

May the voting be light and the clouds like a cruise and the criminal boredom enter the district of hogs.

I love Nowhere where the human brag is a brag of neither time nor place,

But an elephant house of Smithsonian bones and the white cathedrals of grain,

The feeding-lots in the snow with the steers huddled in symmetrical misery, backs to the sleet,

To beef us up in the Beef State plains, something to look at.

Manhole Covers

The beauty of manhole covers—what of that?
Like medals struck by a great savage khan,
Like Mayan calendar stones, unliftable, indecipherable,
Not like the old electrum, chased and scored,
Mottoed and sculptured to a turn,
But notched and whelked and pocked and smashed
With the great company names
(Gentle Bethlehem, smiling United States).
This rustproof artifact of my street,
Long after roads are melted away will lie
Sidewise in the grave of the iron-old world,
Bitten at the edges,
Strong with its cryptic American,
Its dated beauty.

Tornado Warning

It is a beauteous morning but the air turns sick,
The April freshness seems to rot, a curious smell.
Above the wool-pack clouds a rumor stains the sky,
A fallow color deadening atmosphere and mind.
The air gasps horribly for breath, sucking itself
In spasms of sharp pain, light drifts away.
Women walk on grass, a few husbands come home,
Bushes and trees stop dead, children gesticulate,
Radios warn to open windows, tell where to hide.

The pocky cloud mammato-cumulus comes on,
Downward-projecting bosses of brown cloud grow
Lumps on lymphatic sky, blains, tumors, and dugs,
Heavy cloud-boils that writhe in general disease of sky,
While bits of hail clip at the crocuses and clunk
At cars and windowglass.

                              We cannot see the mouth,
We cannot see the mammoth's neck hanging from cloud,
Snout open, lumbering down ancient Nebraska
Where dinosaur lay down in deeps of clay and died,
And towering elephant fell and billion buffalo.
We cannot see the horror-movie of the funnel-cloud
Snuffing up cows, crazing the cringing villages,
Exploding homes and barns, bursting the level lakes.

The Humanities Building

All the bad Bauhaus comes to a head
In this gray slab, this domino, this plinth
Standing among the olives or the old oak trees,
As the case may be, and whatever the clime.
No bells, no murals, no gargoyles,
But rearing like a fort with slits of eyes
Suspicious in the aggregate, its tons
Of concrete, glaciers of no known color,
Gaze down upon us. Saint Thomas More,
Behold the Humanities Building!
                    On the top floor
Are one and a half professors of Greek,
Kicked upstairs but with the better view,
And two philosophers, and assorted Slavics;
Then stacks of languages coming down,
Mainly the mother tongue and its dissident children
(History has a building all its own)
To the bottom level with its secretaries,
Advisors, blue-green photographic light
Of many precious copying machines
Which only the girls are allowed to operate.
And all is bathed in the cool fluorescence
From top to bottom, justly distributed
Light, Innovation, Progress, Equity;
Though in my cell I hope and pray
Not to be confronted by
A student with a gun or a nervous breakdown,
Or a girl who closes the door as she comes in.

The Old Guard sits in judgment and wears ties,
Eying the New in proletarian drag,
Where the Assistant with one lowered eyelid
Plots against Tenure, dreaming of getting it;

And in the lobby, under the bulletin boards,
The Baudelairean forest of posters

For Transcendental Meditation, Audubon Group,
"The Hunchback of Notre Dame," Scientology,
Arab Students Co-op, "Case of the Curious Bride,"
Two students munch upon a single sandwich.

Adult Bookstore

Round the green fountain thick with women
Abstract in the concrete, water trickling
Between their breasts, wetting their waists
Girdled with wheat, pooling in the basin,
The walker pauses, shrugs, peregrinates
To the intersection, section of the city
Where forgotten fountains struggle for existence,
Shops have declined to secondhand
And marginal cultures collect like algae.
Dubious enterprises flourish here,
The massage parlor, the adult bookstore.

Their windows are either yellowed or blacked
Or whited or redded out,
Bold lettering proclaiming No Minors Allowed,
Bachelor Books, Adult Films and Cartoons.

The doorway jogs to the right at a strict angle
And everything from the street is invisible,
Keeping the law and clutching the illusion.
Inside, the light is cold and clean and bright,
Everything sanitary, wrapped in cellophane

Which flashes messages from wall to wall
Of certain interest to the eye that reads
Or does not read: Randy, Coit,
Sex Hold-Up, Discipline, Ghetto Male,
Images of cruelty, ideas for the meek,
Scholarly peeks at French, English and Greek,
And everywhere the more than naked nude
Mystery called the wound that never heals.

Or there a surgical cabinet all glass:
Pink plastic phalli, prickly artifact,
Enlarger finger-small or stallion-size,
Inflatable love partner, five feet four.
Lotions, Hot Melt, super-double-dong,
Battery dildo (origin obscure),

Awakeners of the tired heart's desire
When love goes wrong.

The expense of spirit in a waste of shame
Is sold forever to the single stag
Who takes it home in a brown paper bag.

The White Negress

(Brancusi—Chicago Art Institute)

Who has not seen Brancusi's White Negress?
O quarryman who cut her from the mountain,
Did you see her breathing in the mountain?
Geology, what did you have in mind!

Slightly smaller than life, her head
Stands up like a magnolia bud
In snowy marble,
With a little marble ribbon tying her hair in the back,
Matching her slightly spread nose
And her pretty protruding lips,
The White Negress in all her marble beauty,
So black, so white!

California Petrarchan

I hear the sunset ambulances surround
Suburbia at the turquoise edge of day,
Loping along the not-too-far freeway
Where olive trees and red bloodshed abound.
The oleanders with a shore-like sound
Perform their dance beside my own driveway
As if they also had a word to say
In all their whiteness beautifully gowned.

This Italy with insanity all its own
Lacks only history to make it true
And bitterness that ripens hour by hour.
This baby Italy, more straw than stone,
Stumbling, choking, fighting toward the New,
Bursts into flame with its own fire power.

And Now, the Weather . . .

The rain that ripens oranges
   Will turn to knifey snow
Up on the sawtooth mountains
   Which we can see below.

The rain that fells the almonds
   Will dust the deserts pale
Have intercourse with Denver
   And then will really sail

To Iowa and Nebraska
   And dump its crystal tons
On all its patriotic
   Motherloving sons

Will cross the Appalachians
   Clasp the industrial murk
And lusting for the Apple
   Layer—at last—New York.

Essay on Chess

There are only a few games played by a pair
That are more than games, chess being the most notorious,
Each move signaling an invasion of the other's personality,
        psyche and life-style,
Which is why it is not played by football players,
    truckdrivers
        or housewives
But by students, physicists, auto-didacts and idiot-savants, as
        many Masters are,
And is raised to Olympic status by cultures that hate one
    another,
And can never degenerate to the level, say, of "pingpong di-
    plomacy,"
The contest as iffy as the Big Bang or Plato's Cave.

Hours after a game a lover can say to the defeated,
You were only thinking of yourself, that's why you gave up
        your bishop,
And the other may think, if I lose because I love you
It's not intentional. You are better than I am.
But everything said is just another rorschach.
I need a new racquet, the loser jokes, and will buy a new
    board
Of inlaid wood or cloth-of-silk fit for a rani,
Making it all more formal, like evening dress,
As if it weren't formal enough already.

He muses: I don't want to win from you, I don't want to
    lose
        to you.
My middle game is strong, almost professional,
But at some point you whistle softly and move right
    through;
Damn, ineluctable bitch.

Did you know that before the fifteenth century
The queen could only move one square?

Did you know that the king used to jump all over the place
        before he was hobbled?
A hobby horse. All at once the power was hers.
It happened in Europe when they invented love.

The king stands still. Nobody lays a hand on him.
He just stands still in his mutton-chop whiskers, brainless,
    erect,
Wearing the medals with his own face on them,
His peasants all back in the coffin-box
And a helpless hamstrung horse, ripe for the knackers,
Dying, with crazy beautiful eyes like horse-chestnuts.

He muses: it's only a game invented in Persia
Or some such place that doesn't exist anymore,
And amends this to read—if it were only a game.

The bishops sidle down the avenues, the slippery diplomats
    with
        their penis-heads.
Those moveable castles like panzers, so modern.
And oh the wild horses leaping over the powers,
You can almost see their delicate legs shrouded in pedestals,
Lifted by fingers of gentle giants.

Kings murdered each other over a chessmatch.
It says so in the manuals, and all the chess writers call it
A war-game.
            They call it Errors of Appreciation
In the conventicles of war, by actual generals,
With a freudian assumption of an intention to lose.
To Clausewitz the word was Total War,
To Treitschke A Triumph of National Selfhood fit to
    conquer
        the world,
But all this war talk, Sicilian Defense, the Philador, coign of
        vantage, sphere of action,
The sacrifice, gambit means sacrifice,
All ends in a mate, a word that's not even a pun except in
        English.

Checkmate means *The Shah is dead,*
In chess two queens can never meet,
Two kings can never touch,
And that's the meat of the game, the theory of the play.
The war is only a side-effect of love.

What really matters are the sounds I hear
When you clear the board and put the pieces back in the
    box,
And the verdict of your eyes when you look up at me.

Girls Fighting, Broadway

How beautiful it is,
that eye-on-the-object look.

two girls one blond one latin with fixed hair
in summer dresses hug each other
in a shallow doorway shove each other

as if playfully on streaming Broadway
in heavy August it looks like kissing
to a passerby or some kind of come-on

till a scream retches into the traffic
and heads turn and they are down
on the polluted sidewalk clawing and ripping

and hurling fuck heads striking concrete
thighs open to faces a handsome man
in striped underwear pulls them apart

and is struck backwards a crowd collects
clerks lean out of shops a circle forms
as at a cockfight where feathers fly

and flecks of blood spit through space
they are using teeth and nails and fists
the latin screaming and the blond showing

gold teeth in her open mouth and grabbing
a fallen shoe and swinging hard at
the latin's face they stand they sway they fall

again on the dog-smear and mash of the sidewalk
roiling like lovers spilling over with lust
strong men stand by with burning studious faces

mature women bump their hips to the front
as at a roller-derby while the girls
lurch to their feet between rounds

hissing and panting and heaving in their wet
their passionate pure oblivion

Homewreck

By and large there is no blood,
Police reports to the contrary notwithstanding,
But lots of ichor, a few missing books,
A hasty and disproportionate money transaction
And a sudden enlargement of space.

Three parties form the usual cast,
One happy, one in a rage, and one in the wings,
A telephone rings and rings and rings,
Incinerators open and close and open
And the dramatis personae have all lost face

Though they themselves don't think so
Or try not to think so because the immediate public
Is immediately involved,
Greedy to know what kind of problem is solved
By a seriously departing suitcase.

The public waits for the party in the wings
Who is no longer incognito, who
Has achieved stardom in a matinee
And appears shyly to complete the play
And just as shyly is proferred—an ashtray.

Premises

Moving must be in our nature
    As Heraclitus wrote;
We clamber around the landscape
    Lightfooted as the goat

Taking our premises lightly
    But not our creative acts
Our lares two old typewriters
    But never the artifacts

Which you place around to perfection
    Ensconce them I don't know how
Ceramics and plants and baskets.
    Is the Rothko poster—Horchow?

Aware of the dangers of homing
    Of loading the chambers with crap
We avoid acquisitions like poison
    "Decorating the trap."

May our walls be nunnish, monastic,
    Our only ikon the sky
Except for books by the thousands
    And no *horror vacui*.

The Back

One of the foremost organs of beauty
Especially in women, spaceful and pure
A sky of skin uninterrupted
By mountain-tops and grots
Swamps, fens, rocks, trees
And serpents in gardens: the back.

A roseate fragrance endews it
It gleams like an Australian moon
And is no moor of thatch and thorn
But a mile wide river of veldt
Mile-wide and fraction-deep like the Platte
Where no man lives, a lone terrain,
And luxuriates in itself
And is the very mirage of beauty
To which even whispering is audibly loud
And there are no antries.

On this small platonic continent
Let love graze.

The Spider Mums

The spider mums are yellow
In the chill green room.
Six days from the florist
And standing center stage—
How well they hold their age!

Crystals dropped in water
Perpetuate the bloom
Like Stendhal's twigs of diamonds
Created overnight
Of ancient salt and light.

Essays on time get nowhere
But back where they began.
Still, crystalization
Can be the first in art
Though permanent flowers aren't.

Grant's Tomb Revisited

Something unkempt about it
As if the tomb itself were moribund,
Sepulchre of our own Napoleon,
Litter fluttering under the battleflags
And few white faces.
We've all seen better days,
Hiram Ulysses.
They say the neighborhood is in transition
And only the Hudson keeps an even keel.

The stocky tower rises dirtily,
Imperial, republican,
With sculptures all wrong for today.
I'm puzzled why you like this place.
Pose me under the big stone eagle
Amidst the sociological decay.

Who collared this mausoleum with bright tiles,
Flashing, swooping childwork of the age,
Leaping around like a Luna Park?
Take my picture under the Miró arch,
A neighborhood Miró, not so bad at that.

Let's go upstairs, that's what it's all about
Where only a single guard remains inside
And seems almost surprised to see
Only two visitors, not in a group.

"One million people turned out for the event
"Buildings all over the city draped in black
"Sixty thousand marchers up Broadway
"Stretched seven miles, the President
"Cabinet, Supreme Court, almost the entire Congress
"Ships on the Hudson fired a salute

And there below
The two monogamous crypts

Eight and a half tons each
From the days when there was no doubt
About the reciprocity of might,
The General on the left and Julia on the right.

Impact

High up on the patio window, centered exactly,
suddenly I see in a certain light
the ghost of a bird, like a memorial,
as finely etched as a fossil,
outline of a bird
where it smacked the window hard,
the glass a perfect replica of sky,
thinking it was sky,
the sky that struck it down.

The wings are printed separately,
delicately pointed at either end
like two hummingbirds standing in flight
aimed at each other, past an invisible head
—there is no head—
but the neck is written
and a few body-feathers splayed like tiny fans
and even the legs a parenthesis
and two black blood spots plain as periods.

So that's what it was the child bent over
that the cat was eating,
leaving high up on the patio window
the negative of a bird,
mirage born of a mirage.

The wind has all but washed the feathers away.
The cat is licking its beautiful arrogant leg.

Poet in Residence

for Stuart Wright

To some it's a jewel in the belt of Alma Mater,
To others Beware of the Dog,
To some it's a jetstream from heaven,
To others an acid rain.
> The poet shy and bold as a bullet
> Arrives at his residence
> Booted and spurred but often with tie.
To some that man is patently impossible,
To others potentiality in person.
> The Muse is standing at the open door,
> The poet takes her in his arms.
> Here are the books, she says, here are the beds.
To some he is a danger to the republic,
To others the cause thereof.
> At the window he asks the names of the trees,
> At the window she weeps with open relief.
To some he muddies the conjugation of numbers,
To others he is the decimal.
> She leads him to the extremities of the map,
> To the shores of the immemorial
> For the sake of his residence.
To some he is lost to society forever,
To others society is lost without him.
> The carillons ring in the campus towers at dusk,
> The bats do squareroot over the ivory tower.

The Pigeons

In the denouement of the beautiful storm
A pair of pigeons landed on the ledge
With barely a purchase for their feet,
The female and her mate.
There was no sill
Eleven stories above the street.
They seemed to peer at two small pigeons
Carved of glass, one blue, one green
On the inside, only an inch away.

Is that why they were here
Or were they blown by chance, these doves,
Into a momentary conjunction
By some maker's dream?

The Cathedral Bells

luxury liners laden with souls

I
All day the yellow elevator cage
Rises and falls in the scaffolding
Clutching the biggest cathedral in the world
Like a yellow bee on a climb to a flower
That hasn't opened yet.
The yellow elevator moves at a crawl
To a tower still on the drawing-board.

In morning when I open my eyes I see
The massive cathedral with topless towers
And my heart leaps up, though I'm no christian;
I understand the vocational clamber of bees,
The tired endeavor, not quite in good faith
Since the rich have moved away.

Incredible in this megalopolis of sheerest skyscrapers
To be awakened in the morning by cathedral bells,
Deep bells competing with sixteen-wheeler rigs,
Anger of cop-cars, bleat of ambulances,
Coughing of towering-inferno ladder-trucks.

Returned by such tintinabulations
One half expects to hear a rooster crow
Or a soft drum-roll of rain
Or the slapping of branches, as the giant bells
Outsound even the thrumming of jetplanes
And the pulmonary windmills of helicopters
As the timekeepers of God
Goldenly, leadenly beat out the hours
With a wistful Doppler effect,
And no bell towers visible anywhere,
All very tired, not quite in good faith
Since the rich have moved away.

II

The priest so far away looks like a speck
Under a nave as tall as the *Queen Mary*.
Such immensity must be called-for!
In a minor corner a man is praying in Spanish,
A thousand candles finger the expensive gloom
As in a firstclass dining saloon
Of infinite tables set with silver and lace.
Are we in steerage or in first class?

The entire island sways like a ship,
Slanting its funnels, upping its prow to the moon.
Are we sinking or breaking a transatlantic record?
There seems to be some kind of accord,
A couple of seagulls cruise across the scene
At surveillance height, looking for god knows what,
Blown by the wind, between two rivers.
The speck of a priest tinkles his tiny bell,
Awakening an appetite for wine
In the cathedral of St. John the Divine,
All very tired, not quite in good faith
Since the rich have moved away.

"A Room in Rome"

for Vera Cacciatore

I
The water-poet lay down with flowers above
And the half-sunken boat below his head.
Bitter with young and unrespondent love
Poetry lay foundering on the Italian bed.

Vision and terror held him while he bled
Himself of character and identity.
Upon the coffered ceiling his soul fed
Festoons of roses to his fevered eye.

Friends from afar watch over every breath,
Friends in the room receive his last asides,
Sleep and poetry, charactr'y and death
Stand by the pillow as he outward rides.

Poets of all times and ages come and go
Here where Keats died. The boat sinks on below.

II
The house looks rich; this was no starving poet,
And nowadays a millionaire can't buy it.
The famed boat-fountain lying just below it
Is a bad joke. At least the plash is quiet.

The Spanish Steps sweep upward like a skirt
To the effeminate church that squats on high.
What did he think, lying in mortal hurt,
Of all that grunting in the lovers' sty?

Now he's a library and a sacred name,
Voices take off their shoes when here they tread,
And quite a few remember the belle dame
Who sidewise leant beside his glowing head

When to his healthy friend he turned and said,
Severn, please don't be frightened, and was dead.

Vietnam Memorial

for Liz

It lies on its side in the grassy Mall
A capsized V, a skeletal
Half-sunken hull of a lost cause
Between the Washington Monument and the Capitol.

To see it you descend a downward path
And stare up at the blackened decks of names,
Army of names that holds this cenotaph
Shimmering in shadow in the fosse.

Topside you can hear children at their games,
Down in this trench there is no gab,
Someone lays flowers under a name that was,
Our eyes like seaworms crawl across the slab.

Coasting the fifty-thousand here who died,
We surface breathless, come up bleary-eyed.

Retirement

Something tells him he is off-limits
When he visits the old establishment, maybe for mail.
He still has his key, but it has a slippery feel.
A colleague gives him a startled look, an over-emphatic Hi!
Both act almost as if they'd seen a ghost,
Both know they would rather meet on the street
Than in this particular environment, why
Meeting like this is a kind of misstep.
They wave each other off like a gardener and a bee.
Leaving, he stumbles a little, out of deference,
Hoping he won't run into any Young Turks
(Conversation with them is impossible,
    All idiom and no style).
Meanwhile he keeps coming back to the shop,
A distant cousin, a visitor, a janitor
Whose name is growing harder to recollect.
The word 'posthumous' pops into his head!
Has he joined some sect of the living dead?
After all, he's not some Supreme Court Judge
With unlimited tenure.
Besides, he cherishes his own retirement
And is working at it full time, like a work of art,
Hoping it's nothing as foolish as a hobby
Or as sentimental as a Purple Heart.

At Auden's Grave

From Vienna it's picture postcard all the way.
Where else on earth is such a land at ease!
The fat farms glistening, the polished pigs,
Each carven window box disgorging red
Geraniums, pencil pines and chestnut trees,
The gaily painted tractor rigs,
Steeples with onion domes that seem to say
Grüss Gott, come lie here in our flowerbed.

How many times did Auden take this train
Till that bright autumn day when he was borne
Back in a baggage car after his last
Recital, back to his Horatian house,
His cave of making, now the mask outworn,
The geographical visage consummated,
Back to the village, home to the country man
Without a country, home to the urban bard
Without a city he could call his own.

But suddenly a startling word
Leaps from the signpost of the country lane,
It's AUDENSTRASSE—
The poet becomes a street, the street a poet,
English with German music mated.

Here will arrive no pilgrim mob
As in Westminster Abbey, where his name
Is chiseled next to Eliot's. The sole cab
Has never heard of Auden, has to ask
Gasthaus directions, but we find him there
Ten yards away and settled with his slab,
The bracketed dates, the modest designation,
His plot planted to suffocation
In the country style of *horror vacui*.

Close by, a granite soldier stands
Bareheaded, bowed, without a gun,
Wearing his empty cartridge belt,

A blunt reminder of the First World War,
Signed *Unseren Helden* for those villagers
Who never returned and lay somewhere in France
Entre deux guerres before the next
World War should be begun
By the ultimate twentieth century hun.

Far from his foggy isle
The poety rests in self-exile.
Earth of the great composers of the wordless art
Enshrouds this master of the English tune
Not many miles from where Beethoven scrawled his will
When he could no longer hear the trill
Of the little yellow-hammer, nor the titanic storm.
In such a place Dame Kind
Released the intellectual minstrel's form.

Across the *Audenstrasse* from the grave
A bee drops from the chestnut, sips the beer,
Brings back his image to me, on a day
I bought him a tin collapsible cup to sip
His whiskey from, on some Iowa train,
Knowing his dread of that vertiginous plain.
Now all is comfy in his delectable cave.
I scatter the bee and greet him with my lip.

Whatever commentators come to say—
That life was not your bag—Edwardian—
Misogynist—Greenwich Villager—
Drifter—coward—traitorous clerk—or you,
In your own language, genteel anti-Jew—
I come to bless this plot where you are lain,
Poet who made poetry whole again.

Sandwiched between two families Auden lies,
At last one of the locals, over his grave
A cross, a battle monument, and a name
History will polish to a shine.
Down in the valley hums the Autobahn,
Up here the poet lies sleeping in a vale

That has no exits. All the same,
Right on target and just in time
A NATO fighter rips open the skies
Straight over Auden's domus and is gone.